Published by Creative Education
P.O. Box 227, Mankato, Minnesota 56002
Creative Education is an imprint of The Creative Company

Design and production by Blue Design
Printed in the United States of America

Photographs by Corbis (Bettmann), Getty Images (Brian Bahr, Jonathan Daniel, Stephen Dunn, Elsa, Focus on Sport, Otto Greule Jr, John Grieshop/MLB Photos, Jed Jacobsohn/ALLSPORT, Andy Lyons, JOHN G. MABANGLO/AFP, Ronald Martinez, National Baseball Hall of Fame Library/MLB Photos, Rich Pilling/MLB Photos, Robert Riger, Jamie Squire, Martha Jane Stanton//Time Life Pictures, Rick Stewart, Ron Vesely/MLB Photos, Ofer Wolberger)

Library of Congress Cataloging-in-Publication Data

Richardson, Adele, 1966-
The story of the Houston Astros / by Adele Richardson.
p. cm. — (Baseball: the great American game)
Includes index.
ISBN-13: 978-1-58341-489-7
1. Houston Astros (Baseball team)—History—Juvenile literature. I. Title. II. Series.

GV875.H64R53 2007
796.357'640976414—dc22        2006028716

First Edition
9 8 7 6 5 4 3 2 1

Cover: Pitcher Roger Clemens
Page 1: First baseman Jeff Bagwell
Page 3: Catcher Brad Ausmus

THE STORY OF THE
# HOUSTON
# ASTROS

by Adele Richardson

# THE STORY OF THE
# Houston Astros

**T**he third inning of Game 6 of the 2005 National League Championship Series had just begun, but the score was still 0–0. Then, Houston Astros catcher Brad Ausmus claimed first base with a hit to left field, and shortstop Adam Everett dribbled a ball straight to St. Louis Cardinals second baseman Mark Grudziel-anek, but Everett hustled safely to first. Next, pitcher Roy Oswalt laid down a sacrifice bunt, advancing both base runners and setting the stage for Ausmus to score the first run of the game. The pressure was on now. Up three games to two, the Astros weren't happy just playing in another NLCS—they were determined to win it. Houston had lost the NL pennant the year before to St. Louis,

but this time would be different. Six innings later, the talented squad that had led the Astros into postseason play two years in a row finally earned the 43-year-old franchise its first invitation to the World Series.

# LARGER THAN LIFE

T here is a saying that everything is bigger in Texas, and the city of Houston is no exception. When it was founded in 1836, Houston was barely a dot on the broad map that is Texas. Today, it is a diverse and modern city that boasts the fourth-largest population in the United States. The metropolitan area is home to 5 million residents, 18 Fortune 500 companies, and the largest medical district in the world, the Texas Medical Center. While Houston is a high-rise city with its eyes on the future, its origins are firmly rooted in the past—a past that includes a rich baseball history.

The first known organized ballgame in Houston took place on April 21, 1867. Houston's team, the Stonewalls, annihilated the Galveston Robert E. Lees 35–2. Neither club belonged to any type of formal league, but interest was high, and more than 1,000 people came to watch. It wasn't until 1884 that the Texas League was formed, with teams in Houston, Galveston, Waco, Dallas, Fort Worth, and San Antonio. In 1921, Houston's team was sold to the St. Louis Cardinals and spent more than three decades as a minor-league club. In 1962, Major League Baseball's National League (NL) expanded from 8 to 10 teams, and Houston was granted one franchise, while the other, the Mets, was awarded to New York.

# HOUSTON

The Astros were the second major pro sports franchise to call Houston home, after the Oilers football team.

The new Houston team was named the Colt .45s after the most famous weapon of the Old West. With Harry Craft as manager, the Colts featured a hodgepodge of players acquired through an expansion draft. Fans and players looked forward to opening day against the Chicago Cubs; for a team in its inaugural year, the Colts couldn't have asked for a less threatening first opponent—Chicago hadn't played a .500 season in nine years.

Houston started the game with a bang. The Colts hit a single followed by a triple, scoring their first run before making their first out. Colts right fielder Roman Mejias then slugged two three-run home runs to seal an 11–2 win. For the remainder of the season, Mejias was the Colts' primary source of power, hitting 24 home runs and batting .286. The Colts' pitching, however, was hit-or-miss. Dick "Turk" Farrell, Houston's best pitcher, ended the 1962 season with only 10 wins, and his 3.02 earned run average (ERA) didn't compensate

# THE THREE-PEAT

New ships are traditionally christened with the breaking of champagne bottles on their hulls. The Houston Astros, though, have a tradition of christening new stadiums by winning the first home game. When the Colt .45s played their first major-league game on April 10, 1962, in Colt Stadium, they trounced the Chicago Cubs 11–2. Three years later, the Astrodome became their new home, and the Astros broke in the new ballpark with an exhibition game against the New York Yankees. The game went 12 innings before Houston finally prevailed 2–1. After a couple of decades, the team was in need of a more modern ballpark, and construction began on Minute Maid Park. In 2000, the park (initially called Enron Field) was finished and ready to hold more than 40,000 Astros fans. The team, perhaps wanting to connect with the past, invited the Yankees back for another "first-ever" exhibition game. Yankees outfielder Ricky Ledee earned his team the honor of hitting the first home run in the new park, but it wasn't enough to disrupt Houston tradition. Once again, the Astros pulled out another win in a new ballpark debut, this time needing only nine innings to seal the deal.

for his 20 losses. The team finished 64–96 and in eighth place in the NL.

The Colts fared little better the next two seasons, ending 66–96 both times. The team alternately thrilled and frustrated its fans. Pitcher Ken Johnson threw a no-hitter against the Cincinnati Reds in 1964, but it was the first major-league no-hitter ever thrown that ended in a loss. After Johnson made a bad throw to first base, allowing Reds runner Pete Rose to reach it safely, Rose went on to score the first and only run of the game, and the Reds came out on top 1–0.

The team's home field, Colt Stadium, presented additional problems. Its flamingo-pink general admission seats did not exude professionalism, and the open-air seating invited hordes of mosquitoes to descend upon both fans and players. Unfortunately, when the mosquitoes were tolerable, that meant that the weather was not. Day games were scorching, while night games cooled only to a sticky hot. Fans and players looked forward to the completion of the domed Harris County Stadium, which had been under construction since 1962. Colts owner and former Harris County judge Roy Hofheinz fed the fans' enthusiasm, claiming that the stadium would be "something that will set the pattern for the 21st century. It will antiquate every structure of this type in the world. It will be an Eiffel Tower in its field."

For a very short time, the Astrodome featured real grass and clear ceiling panels that let sunlight into the stadium.

# BASEBALL IN THE EIGHTH WONDER

 **J**udge Hofheinz also called the new "Astrodome" the "Eighth Wonder of the World." And truly, it seemed to be that. At a cost of more than $31 million, the new stadium had a ceiling that rose to 208 feet at its highest point—higher than an 18-story building. It had an internal weather station that kept the temperature at a perfect baseball-playing 71 to 72 degrees, and featured cushioned seats for the fans' comfort. When Houston played its first indoor game in the Astrodome on April 9, 1965, it marked the first time in major-league history that a game had been played inside such a roofed facility.

The move to the Astrodome—which featured not grass, but a synthetic look-alike called AstroTurf—was only one of many changes made before the 1965 season. In an effort to update its image, club owners renamed the team the Houston Astros, a reference to America's space program, which was based in Houston. Players also donned new uniforms that sported a blazing star across the chest.

During their first year in the Astrodome, the Astros' pitching staff was especially strong. Don Wilson recorded two no-hitters, and Larry Dierker became the club's first 20-game winner. But the team's bats had trouble keeping up. Second baseman Joe Morgan was the only real star, setting Astros records for hits (163) and triples (12) and earning NL Rookie of the Year honors.

Then, in the late 1960s, powerhouse outfielder Jimmy "The Toy Cannon" Wynn fired up his bat. Wynn connected for 37 homers in 1967 and 26 more the following year. Especially in the weather-controlled atmosphere of the Astrodome, Wynn consistently crushed the ball. "I just swing the bat," he once explained. He joked that the conditions inside the Astrodome were responsible for his steady pummeling of the ball: "Whenever I come to bat, the wind blows out." Wynn's bat and the accommodating "wind" of the Astrodome helped the Astros enjoy their first .500 season in 1969, the same year the NL was split into two divisions, placing Houston in the NL Western Division.

In 1970 and 1971, the team fell below .500, finishing 79–83 both years. Key trades made in 1971 brought in such players as second baseman Tommy Helms and catcher Jimmy Stewart. Consistent batting and pitching gave Houston its first winning season (84–69) in 1972. Another reason for the newfound success was the addition of star center fielder César Cedeño. The NL soon discovered that the Dominican-born outfielder was a superb base runner, fielder, and hitter. "There must be something Cedeño can't do well," Cincinnati Reds manager Sparky Anderson said, "but I haven't found it yet."

Joe Morgan, who would later gain greater fame with the Cincinnati Reds, was a two-time All-Star in Houston.

JOE MORGAN

## A HARD DAY'S NIGHT

Within the first few innings of the April 15, 1968, game between the Astros and the New York Mets, everyone could see that a pitcher's duel was brewing between the starters—Houston's Don Wilson and New York's Tom Seaver. The game was riddled with groundouts and fly balls, and the only suspenseful action came in the second inning, when Astros catcher Hal King was called out at home. Both starters had been replaced by the 10th inning, but the relievers proved just as tough, and the game was still scoreless and headed into its 20th inning at the Astrodome. At the six-hour mark, both teams were exhausted, and errors began happening more frequently. Then the Mets' Les Rohr made an illegal motion before delivering to home in the 24th, allowing Astros outfielder Norm Miller to advance to second. One groundout later, Miller was on third. The next batter swatted a grounder to Al Weis that rolled through the legs of the Mets' shortstop, and the error cost New York the game. Those 24 innings, played more than 35 years ago, culminated not only in a satisfying win for Houston but also in a club record for the longest game ever.

## PITCHER · J.R. RICHARD

Even though Richard was known to get a little wild on the mound at times, his sizzling pitches baffled many a hitter. Richard routinely hurled 100-mile-per-hour fastballs, and his 94-mile-per-hour sliders usually slipped past whoever stepped up to the plate. During his first game as a starting pitcher, the rookie struck out 15 batters and earned his first win against the San Francisco Giants, blowing pitches by the likes of All-Star outfielders Bobby Bonds and Willie Mays. Richard was seemingly on his way to Hall of Fame status when a massive stroke ended his career in 1980.

**J.R. RICHARD**
**PITCHER**

### STATS

**Astros seasons: 1971–80**

**Height: 6-8**

**Weight: 222**

- **76 career complete games**

- **19 career shutouts**

- **1,493 career strikeouts**

- **107–71 career record**

JIMMY WYNN

**JIMMY WYNN** – Wynn is most remembered for his home run blasts, but speed was a big part of his game as well. He scored 100 or more runs in three seasons with the Astros and set most of Houston's offensive records before leaving town in 1973.

During the 1970s, Houston was determined to become a contender. Sluggers such as third baseman Doug Rader and outfielder Bob Watson had been around since the late 1960s, but the franchise concentrated on beefing up the pitching staff in the new decade. In 1975, hurler J.R. Richard showed potential. The following year, he became the team's second 20-game winner, and in 1978, he set a big-league record by striking out 303 batters.

Knuckleballer Joe Niekro had come on board in 1975 but didn't pitch his best until 1979, when he tallied 21 wins. That year, things started coming together for Houston. The team led the NL West for most of the season until the Reds pulled ahead by a game and a half. Second place was not good enough for these boys of summer, so in the off-season, the Astros acquired strikeout king Nolan Ryan.

## THE WEIRD SEASON

Nearly every ballclub has a season in which the bizarre and unexpected happens. For Houston, 1974 was such a year—filled with oddities, a few lucky breaks, and a sad loss. Opening day found the team in San Diego. Astros third baseman Doug Rader listened to Padres owner Ray Kroc publicly apologize for his team's sorry performance the year before, then Rader criticized Kroc for treating his players "like short-order cooks." Kroc retaliated on June 28, when Houston returned, by calling the game "Short-Order Cook Night." A lucky break was on the menu, though, for a game against the Philadelphia Phillies on June 10. Phillies slugger Mike Schmidt hit a sure home run that sailed 117 feet above the field to hit a speaker hanging from the Astrodome ceiling, but the confused base runners managed to advance only one base before the ball was thrown back in. Houston lost the game 3–0, but the stadium's "helping hand" kept the Astros in it to the end. Near the end of the season, on September 4, Astros pitcher Don Wilson was throwing a no-hitter through eight innings—and losing. Wilson was pulled and ended up losing both the game and the no-hitter. Five months later, he died of carbon monoxide poisoning at his home, adding a tragic footnote to a weird season.

## CATCHER · BRAD AUSMUS

Brad Ausmus spent more than half of his major-league career behind the plate for Houston; the Astros knew a good thing when they saw it, and they kept him there for a reason. The three-time Gold Glove winner was the only catcher in franchise history to earn the prestigious defensive award. While considered a better-than-average hitter for his position, Ausmus was valued primarily for his superior ability in calling games and handling young pitchers. During his first season with the Astros, Ausmus's rocket arm ranked him first among all NL catchers in percentage of base runners caught stealing.

**BRAD AUSMUS**
CATCHER

### STATS

**Astros seasons: 1997–98, 2001–present**

**Height: 5-11**

**Weight: 190**

- **3-time Gold Glove winner**
- **1,408 career hits**
- **652 career runs scored**
- **240 career doubles**

# JOE NIEKRO

Using an effortless throwing motion to toss his famous knuckleball, Joe Niekro won an Astros-record 144 games.

Nolan Ryan made headlines when he joined Houston in 1980, becoming baseball's first $1-million-a-year player.

# POSTSEASON PLAY

lthough they had to fork over a record $1 million-dollar salary to get Ryan from the California Angels, Astros owners found it money well-spent when Ryan hit a three-run home run in only the third game of the 1980 season and achieved his 3,000th career strikeout on July 4. They were also pleased to see their other pitchers performing well. Niekro's knuckleball continued to baffle hitters, and Richard was on his way to having his best season ever on the mound. Cedeño led the team in batting average and stole a whopping 48 bases, and left fielder Jose Cruz was just as big an offensive threat, batting .302 and driving in 91 runs. It seemed that nothing could slow the Astros down. Then tragedy struck.

On July 30, Richard collapsed during warm-ups. He had suffered a stroke that cut off oxygen to the right side of his brain, and it took 18 hours of brain surgery to save his life. Even though Richard was out for the season, his encouraging words bolstered those who remained in the dugout. "I know Nolan Ryan and the rest of the team will never give up on this season," he said. And he was right.

The Astros battled all summer and won the NL West for the first time. In a fiercely tight NL Championship Series (NLCS) against the Philadelphia

## FIRST BASEMAN · JEFF BAGWELL

The label "leader" was firmly attached to this longtime Astros standout as soon as he burst onto the major-league scene in 1991, winning NL Rookie of the Year honors and the club's MVP award. At the plate, Bagwell became the franchise's career leader in home runs, RBI, total bases, extra-base hits, walks, and strikeouts. Being one of only 10 players with at least 400 career long balls and 200 stolen bases set him apart from the pack—and being the only first baseman in major-league history with those numbers made him one of baseball's elite.

**JEFF BAGWELL**
FIRST BASEMAN

### STATS

**Astros seasons: 1991–2006**

**Height: 6-0**

**Weight: 215**

- **449 career HR**

- **1,529 career RBI**

- **4-time All-Star**

- **969 career extra-base hits**

JOSE CRUZ

Sweet-swinging Puerto Rican outfielder Jose Cruz was a quietly steady star in the late 1970s and '80s.

DICKIE THON

Dickie Thon had his greatest season in 1983, hitting 20 home runs, stealing 34 bases, and playing stellar defense.

Phillies, all but one of the five games went into extra innings, but in the end, the Astros lost three games to two.

Houston struggled at the beginning of the 1981 season but was paralyzed by a players' strike that lasted nearly two months. After the strike ended in August, baseball officials decided to split the season so that the winners of the first half would play the winners of the second. Houston's 32–20 second-half record earned it a spot against the Los Angeles Dodgers in the special division playoffs, but just like the year before, the Astros came up short, falling to the Dodgers three games to two.

Houston missed the postseason for the next four years, but fans still witnessed some spectacular baseball. Ryan became baseball's all-time strikeout leader in 1983 and surpassed 4,000 career strikeouts in 1985. The team also

## THE GREAT DEBATE

When Game 4 of the 1980 NLCS began, Houston led the series two games to one over the Philadelphia Phillies; a win that night would have earned the Astros a trip to the World Series. Instead, 1980 became the year that "almost was." During the fourth inning, the Phillies had two runners on base with no outs. Phillies center fielder Garry Maddox popped the ball back to Astros pitcher Vern Ruhle. Ruhle lobbed it to Art Howe at first for the double play. Then Howe saw the runner off second. He ran to the base and tagged Phillies outfielder Bake McBride before McBride could return to second.

completing a rare triple play. Then came the great debate. Home plate umpire Doug Harvey claimed that Ruhle's catch had been a trapped ball, rather than an out, which ignited shouts of protest from the Houston dugout. But the first and third base umpires both said the pitcher caught the ball on the fly, to which the Phillies screamed objections. All six umpires and league president Chub Feeney discussed the play for 20 minutes, but in the end, Harvey ruled it only a double play, insisting that time had been called before Howe's tag at second. Both teams played the remainder of the game under protest.

featured some outstanding fielders such as shortstop Dickie Thon and catcher Alan Ashby. Thon suffered a frightening moment in 1984, when New York Mets pitcher Mike Torrez beaned him in the head, shattering the bone over his left eye. Thon was out for the season and slow to return in 1985. However, he was an integral factor in ensuring a win for Ryan during his 4,000th-strikeout game, contributing three hits and scoring the winning run off a hit by Astros second baseman Billy Doran in the 12th inning. "When Dickie is right," said Doran, "he's the best player on this team. He can do things the rest of us can't."

Although Thon's performance in 1986 wasn't as "right" as it had been before the accident, the rest of the team made up for it. Four Astros pitchers won 12 or more games, and outfielder Kevin Bass and third baseman Denny Walling both ended the season batting over .310. Under rookie manager Hal Lanier, the Astros went 96–66 and returned to the postseason.

They were pitted against the Mets in what had become a best-of-seven NLCS, and by the end of Game 4, the series was tied. During Game 5 in Houston, a blown call at first base denied a run for Houston. The team fought valiantly for 12 innings, but the Mets eventually won. After a marathon 16 innings, Game 6 also went to the Mets, 7–6. Once again, the Astros had come tantalizingly close to their first pennant, only to watch it slip away.

## SECOND BASEMAN · CRAIG BIGGIO

Taking one for the team was a mantra for Craig Biggio, as his 282 hit-by-pitch count ranked second all-time in the majors as of 2006. Though few would admit to the intention, pitchers had good reason to want to plunk Biggio. He was the only player in major-league history to achieve the milestones of 2,800 hits, 600 doubles, 250 home runs, and 400 stolen bases. He was also one of only six players with 104 career steals of third base. His superstitious practice of not changing or cleaning his batting helmet throughout an entire season seemed to pay off for the slugger.

**CRAIG BIGGIO**
SECOND BASEMAN

### STATS

**Astros seasons: 1988–present**

**Height: 5-11**

**Weight: 180**

- **4-time Gold Glove winner**

- **7-time All-Star**

- **637 career doubles**

- **1,776 career runs scored**

ASTROS

**KEVIN BASS** – A switch-hitting outfielder with power, Bass spent eight seasons in Houston in the 1980s and returned for two more in the '90s. His offensive numbers peaked in 1986, when he batted .311 to help carry the Astros to the playoffs.

## THIRD BASEMAN · KEN CAMINITI

Many batters lost infield hits because of Ken Caminiti's laser-like throws to first. In 1987, during his debut game with Houston, Caminiti bashed both a homer and a triple. Multi-RBI games became common for the slugging third-sacker, who compiled 10 games of 5 or more RBI during his career. He struggled with drug abuse throughout his career and afterward, but his death at the age of 41 in 2004 shocked and saddened the baseball community. "He was a warrior in every sense of the word," said Kevin Towers, his former manager with the San Diego Padres

**KEN CAMINITI**
THIRD BASEMAN

STATS

**Astros seasons: 1987–94, 1999–2000**

**Height: 6-0**

**Weight: 200**

- **3-time Gold Glove winner**

- **1996 NL MVP**

- **983 career RBI**

- **3-time All-Star**

# THE SLOW ROAD TO CONTENTION

espite their impressive run at a pennant the year before, the Astros couldn't keep the momentum going into 1987 and beyond. For the next few years, they often stayed in contention until late in the season, when a sudden slide eliminated any chance of postseason play. Consequently, these years also saw many roster changes. As Houston lost big names such as Ryan, Thon, Cruz, and Ashby, rumors began to spread that owner John McMullen was looking to sell the team.

Still, fans were encouraged by the potential of the Astros' newest recruits. Switch-hitting rookie third baseman Ken Caminiti came on board in 1987, and 22-year-old Craig Biggio was placed at catcher in 1988. Rafael Ramirez also began manning shortstop that year, and former player Art Howe took over managerial duties in 1989.

Howe spent his first three years shuffling new players all over the field. Not wanting to waste Biggio's speed behind the plate, Howe moved the young star to the outfield. Left fielder Franklin Stubbs found a new home at first base, and four other players were moved around to difficult positions in 1990.

CRAIG BIGGIO

Craig Biggio spent parts of three decades in Houston, playing catcher and outfield before settling in at second base.

Seven pitchers made their debut on the mound in 1991, and rookie first baseman Jeff Bagwell surprised everyone with his power hitting. Bagwell was not known in the minors for being a slugger, but once he'd been called up to the big leagues, he unleashed his bat and, along with Biggio, led the team in batting average. Even with those two at the plate, the Astros still finished the 1991 season 65–97, in sixth (and last) place in the NL West.

Houston fans will always remember 1994 as the "What If" season. The Astros were switched from the NL West to the NL Central Division, and Bagwell was well on his way to setting club and perhaps major-league home run records when another players' strike lopped the last seven weeks and all of

**JEFF BAGWELL** – Recognized by his red goatee and wide, aggressive batting stance, Bagwell took 449 home run trots in his career. After a spectacular 1994 season cut short by a players' strike, he was awarded both the NL MVP award and a Gold Glove award.

JEFF BAGWELL

## SHORTSTOP · CRAIG REYNOLDS

A native Houstonian, Reynolds spent 11 of his 15 years in the majors with his hometown team. Although an infielder by trade, Reynolds was even used as a pitcher for a total of two innings during his tenure, giving up six hits and seven runs. He made headlines by hitting three triples in one game against the Chicago Cubs on May 16, 1981, which tied a major-league record. Known for his reliability and unselfishness, the steady shortstop led the NL in sacrifice hits in three different seasons.

### STATS

**Astros seasons: 1979–89**

**Height: 6-1**

**Weight: 175**

- **2-time All-Star**

- **1,142 career hits**

- **.256 career BA**

- **377 career RBI**

**CRAIG REYNOLDS**
SHORTSTOP

HOUSTON
ASTROS

## LEFT FIELDER · JOSE CRUZ

From 1975 to 1987, the chant "Cruuuuuuz" was commonplace in the Houston Astrodome. Cruz's lightning-quick speed made him a fan favorite and five-time team MVP during his 13 years with the Astros. A two-time All-Star, the Puerto Rican-born outfielder recorded 26 games with 2 stolen bases. Cruz made getting himself and his teammates back to home look easy. During his time in Houston, he recorded 19 games with 4 or more RBI. Known to fans by his nickname "Cheo," Cruz went on to become the Astros' first base coach.

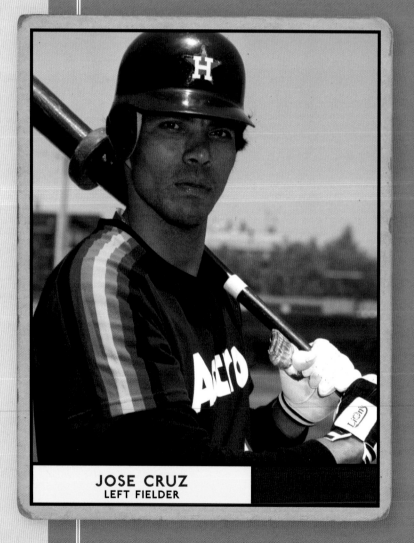

**JOSE CRUZ**
LEFT FIELDER

### STATS

**Astros seasons: 1975–87**

**Height: 6-0**

**Weight: 175**

- **2,251 career hits**

- **1,077 career RBI**

- **317 career stolen bases**

- **Uniform number (25) retired by Astros**

## AGAINST ALL ODDS

Houston's 1999 season was marked by injuries and illnesses. Several key players spent time on the disabled list, but left fielder Moises Alou and rookie catcher Mitch Meluskey were lost for the entire year due to injuries. Then, on June 13, skipper Larry Dierker collapsed in the dugout, and doctors later removed a brain tumor; amazingly, Dierker missed only a month of the season and returned to the helm shortly after the midseason All-Star break. Despite such adversities, many club records were set or tied that season. When Houston's bats came alive, they came alive in a big way. First baseman Jeff Bagwell broke the team's single-season record for walks with 149. He went on to lead the team in homers (42), runs batted in, or RBI (126), and steals (30). Pitcher Mike Hampton recorded 22 wins, and reliever Billy Wagner racked up 39 saves—both club records. In the final half of the year, the Astros set yet another club record with a 12-game winning streak. Although they didn't make it to the World Series, the Astros managed to go 97–65 and stretch their final year at the Astrodome into postseason play, ending their 34-season tenure there with quite a show.

MOISES ALOU

### CENTER FIELDER · CÉSAR CEDEÑO

Manager Leo Durocher predicted that César Cedeño, a 19-year-old Dominican-born rookie at the time, would become the next Willie Mays because of his powerful arm, lively legs, and fearsome bat. Cedeño never achieved Mays's superstar status, but he did achieve some rare feats. He hit for the cycle (hitting a single, double, triple, and home run in one game) twice in his career, and his 550 stolen bases placed him 26th on baseball's all-time list. When Cedeño left Houston in 1981, he was generally regarded as the best all-around player in franchise history.

CÉSAR CEDEÑO
CENTER FIELDER

STATS

**Astros seasons: 1970–81**

**Height: 6-2**

**Weight: 190**

- **5-time Gold Glove winner**

- **4-time All-Star**

- **.285 career BA**

- **22-game hitting streak in 1977**

Derek Bell's steady RBI production helped the Astros win three straight NL Central titles in the late 1990s.

the postseason off the calendar. Houston was in second place going into the strike and showed promise for capturing first, but that dream ended when major league baseball shut down.

The strike left fans feeling bitter, and attendance plummeted all across the majors. The Astros ended 1995 and 1996 in second place, and team owners realized they needed to make big changes in order to regain that crucial fan support. These changes began with Howe's replacement. Houston brass called in Larry Dierker—a colorful television and radio broadcaster and

## RIGHT FIELDER · LANCE BERKMAN

Two weeks after being called up to the majors, Berkman slammed his first two homers, and he never slowed down. The ability to hit well from both sides of the plate placed Berkman in the same class as major-league greats such as Pete Rose and Chipper Jones. Even as he set single-season switch-hitter records for doubles (55) and extra-base hits (94), the All-Star became known for his devotion to children, doing frequent charity work to help underprivileged youth. A native Texan, the laid-back Berkman spent his entire career with the Astros.

### STATS

**Astros seasons: 1999–present**

**Height: 6-1**

**Weight: 205**

- **4-time All-Star**

- **753 career RBI**

- **.304 career BA**

- **.987 career fielding percentage**

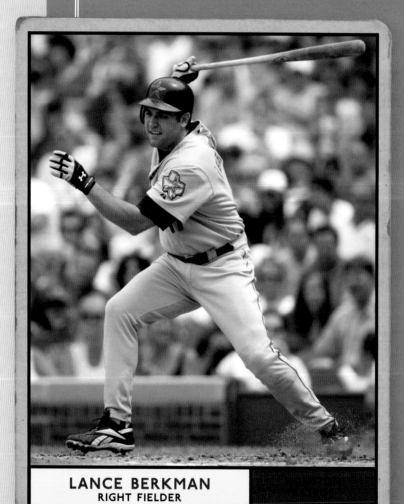

**LANCE BERKMAN**
RIGHT FIELDER

one-time Astros pitcher—to take the helm. Dierker had often commented on what the team was doing wrong while on the air; now he would have the opportunity to correct the Astros' mistakes himself.

Dierker made his debut on April Fools' Day, 1997, but his appointment was no joke. Dierker guided the team to first place in the NL Central that season, and Houston then faced the Atlanta Braves for a shot at the NLCS. The Braves, however, brought dynamic pitching and red-hot bats to the NL Division Series (NLDS), quieting the Astros and their top hitters—Bagwell, Biggio, and right fielder Derek Bell, collectively known as "The Killer B's." "Our offense sputtered," Bagwell conceded. "We just didn't score enough runs. . . . But this should give us momentum going into spring training. Now we have unfinished business."

# HOME RUN DERBY

The Home Run Derby has been a popular segment of the annual All-Star Game for more than two decades. Although the Astros and Chicago Cubs were not playing in an All-Star event on September 9, 2000, Houston players seemed focused on the long ball. Astros shortstop Tim Bogar was the second man to bat in the game and the first to slam one over the ivy-covered wall in Wrigley Field that day—his first of two homers in the game. Astros center fielder Richard Hidalgo connected with the sweet spot in both the third and eighth innings

and right fielder Lance Berkman got in on the act as well. He blasted a pitch into Wrigley's bleachers late in the fourth inning and repeated the feat with another homer in the eighth. By the end of the fourth, left fielder Daryle Ward was the only Astros outfielder without a homer—a situation he remedied shortly after stepping to the plate in the seventh inning. The Astros pounded the Cubs 14–4 that day. Over nine innings, they sent 45 hitters to the plate and went through five Cubs pitchers, setting a new club record with seven homers in one game.

# PENNANT FEVER

he Astros' agenda for 1998 was to finish what they had started. To accomplish this, they added two players: left fielder Moises Alou and pitcher Randy "The Big Unit" Johnson. With Alou's 124 RBI and Johnson's 100-mile-per-hour fastballs, the Astros blew through the competition and again won the NL Central. But this NLDS had the same outcome as the previous year's, with Houston losing to the San Diego Padres in four games.

In 1999, Houston repeated its first-place finish in the NL Central. Helping spark the team was young outfielder Lance Berkman, who quickly displayed rare home run power. As in 1997, the team's opponent in the NLDS was the Braves. And like the last time, the Astros could not pull off the win. The team hoped for a boost playing in the new Enron Field (later renamed Minute Maid Park) in 2000 but didn't get it, finishing well out of playoff contention.

With Berkman in right field batting an impressive .331 and Wade Miller pitching well, the 2001 Astros returned to the NLDS. But in what was getting to be a frustrating pattern, Houston was bested by Atlanta in three games. "It's a recurring theme, no question about it," Bagwell said. "We got down in a little hole, and we were never able to dig ourselves out."

Lance Berkman was a rarity—a slugger with a keen batting eye. Through 2006, he carried a career .304 average.

LANCE BERKMAN

Disheartened by the team's continuing playoff stalls, Dierker turned over the managerial reins to Jimy Williams. The Astros fell from atop the division, finishing in second place in 2002 and 2003. But 2004 was a different story. With a roster that now featured slugging outfielder Carlos Beltran and star pitchers Andy Pettitte and Roger Clemens, Houston made the playoffs and topped its old foes in Atlanta to meet the St. Louis Cardinals in the NLCS. The Astros and Cardinals battled fiercely throughout the first six games, forcing a deciding Game 7. Houston scored runs in the first and third innings but gave up three in the sixth inning to lose 5–2. Once again, the Astros' long-awaited trip to the "Fall Classic" was put on hold.

New manager and former Astros infielder Phil Garner had a lot to deal

**ROGER CLEMENS** – Although he was a 41-year-old baseball legend by the time he joined the Astros in 2004, Clemens was still an ace. In his first season in his native state of Texas, the big right-hander went 18–4 and won his seventh career Cy Young Award.

## MANAGER · LARRY DIERKER

When Larry Dierker left his 18-year television and radio broadcasting position with the Astros to become the team's manager in 1997, many people were surprised at the hiring. Despite the doubters, Dierker never wavered in his steadfast strategy, leading his team to four playoff appearances in five years. His .556 winning percentage made him the most successful skipper in team history, and he earned the 1998 NL Manager of the Year award after the Astros went 102–60. Prior to broadcasting and managing, Dierker spent 13 seasons as a pitcher with the franchise, recording a no-hitter in 1976.

### STATS

**Astros seasons as manager: 1997–2001**

**Height: 6-4**

**Weight: 215**

**Managerial Record: 435–348**

**NL Central Titles: 1997, 1998, 1999, 2001**

**LARRY DIERKER**
MANAGER

CARLOS BELTRAN

Carlos Beltran made baseball history in the 2004 playoffs, slugging eight home runs in the NLDS and NLCS.

Roy Oswalt put himself among the greatest of Astros pitchers with 20-win seasons in both 2004 and 2005.

with in 2005. Both Berkman and Bagwell missed a month with injuries, and the flu virus spread through the clubhouse, putting a third of the roster out of commission. Against all odds, Houston went 89–73 and beat the Braves in the NLDS and the Cardinals in the NLCS to earn the right to square off against the Chicago White Sox in the World Series. They were no match for the red-hot Sox, though, losing the series in four straight games.

The Astros slumped to 82–80 the following season, but with a loaded roster that included Berkman, pitcher Roy Oswalt, closer Brad Lidge, and newly signed outfielder Carlos Lee, Houston figured to remain a top contender in the highly competitive NL Central. "I think that whoever plays well within the division is going to have a good shot at the pennant," Garner said as the 2007 season kicked off.

From their days as the sharp-shooting Colt .45s, to their seasons in the Eighth Wonder of the World, to their 2005 World Series appearance, the Houston Astros have had a monumental history that has been marred only by never having won a World Series. Now, after several close calls, today's Astros are determined to soar into the rarified air of the World Series once again. And this time, they plan to win it all.